BIOMES
of the World™

DESERTS
The Living Landscape

Robert Greenberger

rosen publishing's
rosen
central®

New York

Published in 2009 by The Rosen Publishing Group, Inc.
29 East 21st Street, New York, NY 10010

Library of Congress Cataloging-in-Publication Data

Greenberger, Robert.
Deserts: the living landscape / Robert Greenberger.
    p. cm.—(Biomes of the world)
Includes bibliographical references.
ISBN-13: 978-1-4358-5005-7 (library binding)
ISBN-13: 978-1-4358-5431-4 (pbk)
ISBN-13: 978-1-4358-5437-6 (6 pack)
1. Desert ecology—Juvenile literature 2. Deserts—Juvenile literature.
I. Title.
QH541.5.D4G74 2009
577.54—dc22

                                                    2008025212

Manufactured in the United States of America

On the cover: (Inset) An agama lizard in its desert habitat. (*Background*) desert sand dunes.

CONTENTS

INTRODUCTION

Our planet is an ecosystem, with interrelated geography, geology, and life. Each affects the other. The subsection pertaining to organic life-forms can also be called a biome.

Earth has six clearly identified biomes from the tundra to the desert, all unique in their composition. The desert, for example, receives a tenth of the rainfall that the rain forest receives and, as a result, the kinds of life both support are vastly different. Also distinct are the dangers each biome faces as global warming changes the very way nature works.

The desert may be the most extreme example of a biome because most people think of it as hot and arid, an inhospitable environment for man, animal, or plant life. Of course, the truth is very different. The desert is home to all manner of living beings, most of which have adapted to their surroundings and are quite comfortable in their natural habitat.

The word "desert" is derived from the Latin word *desertum*, meaning "unpopulated place," and is said to be traced back to an Egyptian word that translates to "red land." Given the reddish soil on Mars, which has proven to be mostly desert, it's an apt description.

A man walks along the vast desert known as an erg in Morocco.

Deserts are also like living beings, moving their borders all the time, a process most know as desertification. Drying conditions turn other biomes into desert. Rather than expand the amount of the earth that is desert, they just relocate their boundaries.

One benefit to the desert landscape, which receives the least precipitation of the six biomes, is that history has been more easily preserved, allowing researchers to understand how our planet was formed and has changed through the millennia. Its hard, unforgiving surface has also allowed scientists to test new vehicles, from high-performance race cars to the space shuttle. The desert's clearer atmosphere also makes for ideal conditions for studying the stars to learn about our planet's place in the universe.

In the pages ahead, you will learn how the deserts were first formed, how they support life, and how changes to the world at large may change the deserts in the years to come.

CHAPTER 1

THE DESERT BIOME

To most people, the word "desert" conjures up a vast area with a scorching sun and sand dunes as far as the eye can see. The reality is that there are many different types of deserts, and they can be found on every continent, even Antarctica. According to the National Air and Space Administration (NASA), Earth's deserts can be found between 15° and 35° latitude— north and south of the equator and in broad stretches at 20° to 30° north and south of the equator, along the Tropics of Cancer and Capricorn.

Deserts were first formed as a result of Earth's rotation on its axis. The equator is where the planet is at its hottest, and the heated air spreads both north and south, cooling the farther it travels. As it cools and condenses, moisture is formed and the rainfall creates the planet's tropical zones. In addition to temperature, the air also has pressure. That pressure is lower at the equator than farther north or south. The higher-pressure areas force the air to sink toward the surface; such motion creates wind. There exist two subtropical, high-pressure belts of air that blow hot and virtually moisture-free. It's these winds that helped form the vast deserts, such as the Sahara in Africa.

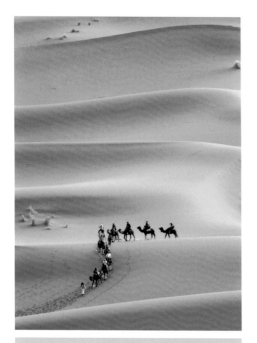

A camel caravan moves through the Sahara Desert in Africa.

Lack of Rainfall

Just as there are regions that get high rainfall, there are opposite areas that receive almost no rainfall throughout the year. It's these areas that form the deserts around the world. As some of these winds travel across the land, they lose moisture, as happens with the winds arriving in the middle of the Sahara. Mountains can also absorb moisture from the winds, so what reaches the flatter land in as little as 100 miles (161 kilometers) is dry air. With such little rainfall, as little as 10 inches (25 centimeters) a year, the vegetation that thrives is the type that requires little water, such as cacti and short grass. Most of the land, though, is bare soil, resulting from eolian deflation, that is, the process of wind removing the finer grains of sand. What's left includes pebbles and exposed bedrock, along with desert lakes and oases. The temperature ranges from an average high of 100.4 degrees Fahrenheit (38 degrees Celsius) to a low of 24.98° F (–3.9° C) at night.

As scientists studied the world, it became obvious that the deserts were not all the same. It wasn't until 1953, however, that a man named Peveril Meigs came up with a classification system. He divided the planet into thirds based on the annual precipitation that deserts received. Deserts are actually considered drylands, earning the name from their arid nature and the fact that several actually lose moisture over a twelve-month period. "Dryland" is the term

used by many scientists and is accepted by the United Nations as the umbrella classification. Drylands have three components: extremely arid deserts, arid deserts, and semiarid deserts. Extremely arid deserts are ones that have a minimum of twelve consecutive dry months. Arid deserts receive less than .820209 feet (.25 meters) of annual rainfall. Semiarid lands receive between .820209 feet (.25 m) and 1.64 feet (.5 m) of rainfall a year. The first two categories are considered deserts, while the semiarid regions are known as steppes.

Another factor that comes into play when determining a desert is the rate of evaporation and area temperature. For example, the Brooks Range in Alaska receives less than 10 inches (25 cm) of rainfall but is not recognized as a desert.

These are the vast sand dunes of the Skeleton Coast in Walvis Bay, Namibia. They show that desert and ocean can exist side-by-side.

SAND DUNES

When thinking about the desert, one imagines sand dunes. But there are many different kinds of dunes, starting with barchan dunes. Barchan dunes are shaped like crescents and are formed from strong winds. Seif dunes are shaped in the same direction as the wind blowing along longitudinal lines. Transverse dunes occur at right angles to the wind, while star dunes have ridges flaring out from a central point.

Given their creation through wind, dunes are not stationary but nomadic, following the weather patterns. One method is called saltation, where the wind effectively skims the sand, knocking other particles and moving the mass. If the winds are strong enough, sandstorms are created and the landscape is effectively altered once the storms end. As a result, dunes can threaten animal enclaves or human settlements. In 2002, for example, 144 Iranian villages were buried during sandstorms, leaving the people homeless.

Where the Deserts Are

Deserts are normally found in landlocked areas, away from sources of moisture. However, there remain deserts, including the Atacama in Chile, that are coastal. They are always on the western coast. These are considered coastal fog-deserts with arid conditions caused by cold ocean currents. Following this definition, about one-quarter of Earth's land, about 20,940,209.2 sq miles (33.7 million sq km), is desert.

The land wasn't always this way, but Earth changed gradually through the years. The amount of the earth that is a desert has

changed through the eras, such as the glacial period more commonly called the ice age. Over the past five thousand years, the planet's trend has been to warming and aridization.

Another common element to the desert is the oasis, which is a pocket of water, usually a spring that brings about a different form of vegetation and helps feed animal life. Humans usually build encampments or towns around the life-giving water supply.

The moisture that does fall in the desert does not drip down but arrives via storms. When the water comes rushing down from the sky, it runs along previously dug channels, known as arroyos or wadis. Even with these pathways, they can quickly overflow and create a flash flood.

Water in the Desert

Deserts are not entirely devoid of water throughout the year either. After all, the famed Nile River runs through the Sahara in Africa, and the Colorado River runs through North American deserts. Each moves such vast amounts of water that even after evaporation from the heat and moisture-free atmosphere, there is plenty to flow from end to end. The rivers also carry important sedimentary materials along their beds and to the oceans they feed, all contributing to the global ecosystem.

A Felucca cruises down the Nile River in Egypt. The Sahara Desert can be seen in the background.

There are even desert lakes, which can be formed when deep basins exist and trap vast quantities of water that also exceed the evaporation rate. These can be fed from rain or snowmelt from nearby mountain ranges. Despite the lake designation, they tend to be shallow and salty— not at all good for sport or leisure. Smaller lakes tend to dry up now and then, leaving salty deposits that harden into a crust called hardpan. The dry lake bed is then known as a playa. Many playas dot North America and can be traced back to when they were active lakes during the last ice age, dating to more than twelve thousand years ago.

These hardened lands are where automobiles and airplanes can be tested and where the space shuttle usually lands in California upon its return from orbit. The Bonneville Speedway in Nevada is a noteworthy location where speed records have been continually set since the 1950s.

The repeated cycles of precipitation and evaporation have led to concentrated mineral deposits being formed in the ground, allowing man to mine the land for copper, lead-zinc, uranium, boron, gypsum, sodium chloride, and borates, among many others. In South America's Atacama Desert, sodium nitrate has been continually mined for use in explosives and fertilizers.

Petroleum, one of the most vital materials, has also been preserved deep under these deserts. The Middle Eastern oil fields remain a vital energy resource for many countries and millions of workers, not to mention consumers around the globe who need its by-products, including gasoline and plastics.

Desertification

While air pressure and wind help form deserts, man's worldwide activities have led to a disastrous condition known as desertification. While land has been transformed through irrigation in one area, it leaches needed water from other areas, drying them out and turning them into drylands. One of the best known examples of rapid

Desertification occurs over time when land, such as this in Madagascar, is stripped of its plant life and is not reseeded.

desertification was the transformation of America's Great Plains into the Dust Bowl during the Great Depression of the 1930s. It took a massive change in how the land was irrigated and farmed to restore the land for agricultural use. A decade later, China experienced a similar problem.

These changes to the ecosystem threaten plant and animal life. Semiarid lands lose moisture and become arid, forcing grasses to become shrubs that cannot sustain life. In Madagascar alone, a tenth of the country's land has been rendered useless through desertification. In Africa, the Institute for Natural Resources in Africa (INRA) estimates that if changes are not made, the continent will only be able to feed a quarter of its population by 2025.

Cold Deserts

Say "desert" and you think of hot, arid land. But there are cold deserts, too. These can be found where the climate produces snow instead of rain during the winter months of a region. The snow is caused by moist air cooling as it moves up a mountain. The cool air means the atmosphere holds less moisture and it falls as snowflakes. The area also never gets warm enough to support sustained plant life. Wildlife—such as the badger, kit fox, and coyote—survives by burrowing underground to keep warm.

On maps, cold deserts can be found 30° latitude both north and south of the equator, therefore in the Antarctic, Greenland, and the Nearctic realms, which will be described in the next chapter.

CHAPTER 2

THE DIFFERENT KINDS OF DESERTS

The heat in a desert can reach a high of 134° F (56° C) in a place like North America's Death Valley, but people will tell you it's bearable because it's a dry heat. The air tends to only have between 10 and 20 percent humidity.

While true, the heat can sap a person's energy, burning the skin. If a person is left exposed, the heat can kill that person. People in these conditions can lose one quart of water an hour through perspiration. If this water is not replenished, a person can become ill.

Deserts tend to be flatlands, meaning there's little shade to provide relief and the sun blankets the land, which readily absorbs its heat. Without plentiful moisture to help absorb the sun's radiation, the dry air is a poor filter. Similarly, the ground is porous, letting the heat right back out after the sun sets. At night, though, with nothing to hold on to the heat, the hot lands quickly radiate the heat back into the sky, and the area rapidly cools off. A day may peak at 103° F (39° C) and reach a low of 49° F (9° C).

Whenever there are communities built in the desert, the artificial constructions help alter that ebb and flow of heat, moderating the daily swings between high and low temperatures.

The dry air can be whipped into high winds creating dust devils, which are similar to tornadoes. They help remake the desert landscape in mere minutes.

Desert Names

Just as Alaskans have many names for snow, desert dwellers can differentiate the wind with names such as harmattan, santana, khamsin, and sirocco. Some of these winds can be harsh enough to peel paint off of cars and reshape the landscape in a day. The fiercest winds earn names like whirlwind or dust devil, spinning across the barren land in concentrated form, similar to twisters, but remaining in the desert and causing little destruction.

The resulting topography can contain fresh flatlands and new collections of sand dunes. Some of these dunes, known as ergs, are

just a small percentage of deserts, while the vast majority of the surface is flat, hard ground.

The few oases of water and vegetation have existed since the planet first cooled. They helped determine the paths Homo sapiens used when searching for food or shelter. These became the first trade routes and helped shape civilization.

The World Wildlife Fund (WWF) divided the world into ecozones, most of which have deserts as part of their makeup. The only ecozone without a desert is Oceania, which includes Polynesia, Fiji, and Micronesia.

- **Afrotropic** Located in the portions of Africa below the Sahara, such as the Horn of Africa and Madagascar.
- **Australasia** Includes New Zealand, New Guinea, and surrounding islands. Australia itself has a desert in the continent's interior. The desert covers 1.39 million square miles (3.6 million sq km).
- **Indomalaya** Is found in South and Southeast Asia, with just two lowland deserts—the Indus Valley and Thar. This is the smallest region covering just 100,386.56 square miles (0.26 million sq km), but it has the highest proportion of humans living on the land.
- **The Nearctic** Located in North America, these deserts cover 424,712.38 square miles (1.7 million sq km). Three of the four major deserts are located between the Rocky Mountains and the Sierra Nevadas—the Sonoran, Mojave, and Great Basin. These have warm seasons and a hot summer, receiving little rainfall, about 11 inches (28 cm) a year. The winds leave the remaining soil coarse, allowing for good drainage to support life.

People living in the desert often follow a nomadic lifestyle, going from oasis to oasis in search of food and water.

- **Paleartic** Located in Eurasia and Northern Africa. The largest deserts here include the Sahara and Arabian deserts, covering 6,177,634.56 square miles (16 million sq km), totaling 63 percent of the planet's deserts. The Sahara alone covers 10 percent of Africa.
- **Montane deserts** Highland areas located below the tree line, mostly in Central Asia, which has the most varied landscape as opposed to flat deserts, and contains bodies of water like the Caspian Sea. The high altitudes

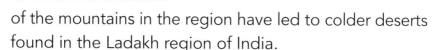

of the mountains in the region have led to colder deserts found in the Ladakh region of India.

- **Neotropic** Includes South and Central America, the Mexican lowlands, the Caribbean islands, and southern Florida. While it contains more tropical rain forests than any other part of the world, it also has deserts found through South America, including Chile, Peru, Brazil, and Mexico.

- **Antarctic** Includes the continent of Antarctica and nearby islands, such as the South Sandwich Islands, South Orkney Islands, the South Shetland Islands, Bouvet Island, the Crozet Islands, the Kerguelen Islands, and the McDonald Islands.

CHAPTER 3

LIFE IN THE DESERT

Despite their barren appearance, deserts are as alive with plant and animal life as any other biome. They have had to adapt to their surroundings, given the spare water supply and high temperatures. Different deserts and regions have given rise to varied life-forms, each contributing to their ecologies.

Plant Life

Plants found in the desert are not very tall. Instead, they hug the ground, surviving on what water they manage to tap underground or absorb during the brief rainy season. These are largely known as xerophytes. As a result, they do not offer much in the way of shade to insects, animals, or man. Instead, the plants are designed for long-term survival and tend not to be tasty as food or good for burning as fuel.

The leaves and stalks that compose most desert life are designed to conserve water under their thick coats. A common example would be the spiky cactus, of which there are many varieties. They have thorns, not leaves, and within the thick skin is water stored for them to survive on between storms. The thorns and thick epidermis also protect the plants from predatory life.

Plants also provide shelter for other desert life. For example, the saguaro cactus is large enough to shelter birds in the Sonoran Desert.

Although cacti are often thought of as characteristic desert plants, other types of plants have adapted well to the arid environment. They include the plants belonging to the pea and sunflower families.

Most plant life limits the surface area exposed to the harsh sun, minimizing the evaporation rate. Some plants have glossy leaves to radiate the heat and light, while others have a waxy coating to prevent moisture loss.

Water can be stored in leaves, roots, or stems, depending on the plant. Such plants are described as succulents. Most have long taproots that can reach more than 20 feet (60.1 m) deep underground and find the local water table. Such long roots also ensure plants are well anchored for whenever the winds reach storm levels. The root systems help control the ecosystem's rate of erosion, while the plants themselves help break the wind and protect surface life.

There are some plants that have horizontal root systems that are located shallowly beneath the surface and extend far from the plant itself. As rain falls, the roots capture the water as quickly as it sinks into the soil.

The saguaro cactus can grow very tall, as seen by this one found at Saguaro National Park, Arizona.

ADAPTATIONS

To endure the brutal heat, plants produce hard-shelled seeds for reproduction. Once the hard rains come, they quickly germinate, grow, and produce new seeds for the next generation. As a result, the new plant life is prepared to absorb its own water supply. Some plants count on the wind to help spread the seeds to avoid clustering too close together and essentially fighting for the same water supply. Plants are also salt-tolerant, given the high potassium content in many deserts.

One unique method of water capture is that of the Australian mulga tree. *Mulga* is an Aboriginal term for "shields." The tree's tiny leaves grow facing upward so that rainfall is captured in them, funneling the liquid toward the tree's trunk and then down to the center, where the roots are concentrated in the ground.

Gas Exchange

While plants continue to experience photosynthesis, how they exchange gases can vary. Plants including the yucca, ocotillo, turpentine bush, prickly pear, false mesquite, sotol, ephedra, agave, and brittlebush perform photosynthesis during the cooler night with the day's lowest evaporation rate. They open stomata—tiny openings in their skin—to absorb and process oxygen.

In addition to plant life, such as the cactus, varying forms of short grass can be found in most desert environments. Accompanying them would be bushes and sagebrush, all designed to withstand the heat and lack of moisture. Each desert boasts its own unique

The prickly pear cactus flower has thorns that capture the water, which is then stored within the thick plant skin.

life-forms, such as the saguaro cactus, which is only found in the Sonoran Desert, or the spinifex in the Australian desert.

Most plants are built to withstand the winds, but how they do it can vary. For example, the creosote bush looks thin and spindly but allows the wind to pass right through its branches. Buckwheat will stretch its central stem to keep its head over the ground wind, and it can be some 15 feet (4.57 m) above ground. Sagebrush will let itself be blown with the wind, depositing seeds as it rolls along.

Another consequence of adaptation is that many plants and animals tend to live longer. The saguaro can live as long as two hundred years, developing very slowly. It takes them nine years just to reach 6 inches (15 cm) in height. Their first branches don't arrive until they are seventy-five years old. At full growth, they can be 49 feet (15 m) tall, weighing up to 10 tons (10,000 kilograms).

Animal Life

Deserts are rife with a wide variety of insect and animal life, all adapted for the brutal conditions.

The adaptations vary but usually involve ways to withstand the worst of the heat and bright sunlight. Toads, for example, will dig burrows and then secrete a gelatinous substance to coat themselves. They fall into torpor for as long as nine months until the heavy rains arrive. Other amphibians have accelerated life cycles, like the plants, to enhance their survival. Some eggs, such as those of the fairy shrimp, remain dormant until the environment reaches an optimal stage.

Another adaptation is that the animals' hunting and active cycles are set during the cooler evening hours, while the animals sleep during the harsh daylight hours. These animals tend to burrow for sleeping spaces during the daytime, emerging to eat, play, and mate at night. Various insects, arachnids, reptiles, birds, and mammals all do this.

Animals will follow the normal food chain dynamics and eat smaller animals or insects or plants and their seeds. Some animals require such little water that they get what they need from their food and forgo drinking from freshwater supplies even when they are available.

Similarly, there are animals that have developed glands allowing them to secrete salt without losing water. Those that lack sweat glands tend to also have concentrated urine and body fat. A camel, for example, does not have water in its hump but, rather, fat, which it stores to live off of during lean times. Many animals, including reptiles, have very little body fat at all, cutting down on body heat.

Other Creatures

Birds cannot burrow, so they seek shade between rocks or under low-lying bushes. They also avoid the worst of the heat radiating off

Popularized on American television, a suricate, or meerkat, family huddles together in Kalahari, South Africa.

the hard surfaces by going to higher altitudes, where the air is cooler. Birds, like dogs, cannot sweat, so they pant or flutter to remove heat. Some birds will eat flesh and get their moisture from their prey, while seed-eating birds must remain near sources of water.

The desert is also home to insects, starting with harvester ants, which gather plant seeds and live off of them during the dry season. There are also honeypot ants. In their colonies, selected members eat big amounts of sugar, growing too large to move and ultimately providing sustenance to the remainder of the colony.

Arachnids, including spiders and scorpions, also thrive in the desert. Scorpions have their infamous poison-tipped tails that can paralyze their prey, thus giving scorpions an advantage.

Here is the frilled lizard in defensive mode, looking larger to scare off predators.

It's the reptiles, though, that are among the most interesting species found in the desert. Snakes of all sizes and varieties can control their body temperatures, allowing them to withstand both the daytime heat and the nighttime cold. The snakes and lizards are cold-blooded creatures making them well equipped for the environs. Many lizards can camouflage themselves, changing color to blend in with their environment. Other species can change their shape to ward off predators. One example is the frilled lizard, which can open its mouth and expand the surrounding frill, making it appear larger and more threatening than it truly is.

Reptiles of all varieties have scaly skin to allow movement across the terrain in addition to conserving moisture. Many have been designed to use their environment to either shed or absorb heat, letting them conserve energy. This requires less movement and less need for food and water.

Man

The desert ecosystem tightly relies on managing its resources to sustain all manner of life. What little water there is must be harvested and retained by plants and animals alike. They have to be prepared to handle the heat or wind and relocate as the terrain changes.

It's no different for the men and women who live in the desert. Their skins are darker to handle the sunlight and heat, and most people have developed nomadic lifestyles to go from oasis to oasis to find food and drink. Those exposed to the elements can easily be

Believe it or not, there are deserts in cold climates. Here, an Inuit is ice fishing in Nunavut, Canada.

dehydrated and die within a single day, depending upon the sun's strength.

The United Nations estimates some five hundred million people live in the desert, making up only 8 percent of the total human population. The hot, arid land of Africa and the Middle East is also considered the cradle of civilization and where the Jewish, Christian, and Islamic faiths were founded.

Just as plant and animal life have adapted to the environment, so have the people. The African Topnaar tribe is known for their exceptional knowledge of local plants and animals. Others have managed to domesticate animals and even farm. The great Egyptian empire rose four thousand years ago, thriving despite its desert environs. In North and South America, the Pueblo people also managed substantial civilization, despite the unfavorable conditions. People survive and even thrive in cold deserts. One example is the Inuit people of Alaska.

CHAPTER 4

ENVIRONMENTAL IMPACT

Mankind has spread across the planet, and its development of mechanized methods for agriculture and manufacturing over the past three centuries has led to a condition known as global warming. In addition to the planet growing warmer, there have been dramatic environmental effects, even in places that were hot to begin with, including the desert.

In 2005, *National Geographic* magazine reported that Africa's Kalahari dune fields will experience dramatic changes, as rainfall has declined, droughts have lengthened, and windstorms have grown more powerful. The desert there measures 1 million square miles (2.5 million sq km) from northern South Africa to Zambia. It is part of the 25 percent of Africa that is covered in dunes.

"This could have major consequences for several states and for the people who farm the land in these areas," said David Thomas, a physical geographer at Oxford University in England who participated in a study. While most people equate global warming with the loss of ice caps and shrinking glaciers, it has had other effects as well.

The Kalahari and other dune-filled deserts around the world are largely stable because of the vegetation that helps anchor the dunes and sand. As drought increases, the vegetation is weakened and thus becomes more susceptible to being displaced by windstorms, which in turn could change the dunes' locations. Additionally, the drier air and harsher winds could combine to further erode the land, spreading the boundaries of a desert region in a process known as desertification.

The Hardest Hit Areas

A United Nations report suggests that Australia's Great Victoria Desert, South America's Atacama, and North America's Colorado Great Basin will suffer the most. On the other hand, the Gobi Desert is expected to see annual rainfall increases of between 10 and 15 percent by the end of the century.

Rain in the Gobi Desert is rare. But that may change as global warming alters weather patterns.

Oxford's Norman Myers researched the phenomenon and predicted that some two hundred million people will become "climate refugees" by 2050. Developments have already begun, including in Brazil, where one in five people born in the arid northeast has relocated to avoid drought. Three provinces in China are seeing people move as the Gobi Desert spreads out. In Nigeria, some 1,250 square miles (2,000 sq km) of land is turning into desert every year, forcing people to relocate for survival.

The study David Thomas participated in used computer models to project what will happen to the Kalahari based on the current changes to the erodibility of the soil and dunes, and the erosivity, which measures the wind energy involved in dune erosion.

Global warming had resulted in floods in the Darbhanga district of northern India in August 2007.

"We found that as the century progressed, the dune fields of the mega-Kalahari reactivate, partly due to erodibility increasing as precipitation declines, and partly as wind energy increases, especially toward the end of the dry season when surfaces are least vegetated," Thomas told *National Geographic*.

Their computer models indicated that the dune fields in Botswana and Namibia will be the first to be affected, by 2040, while the dunes in Angola, Zimbabwe, and Zambia will start their shift by 2070. In some ways, these dunes will spread and move in ways not seen in Africa in some fourteen thousand years. Livestock farming, currently a staple in the region, would be almost impossible as conditions worsen, making life for people more difficult.

"These are areas where dunes are currently wooded in many places. We'll potentially see major environmental changes [with] currently vegetated but sandy landscapes reverting to active, blowing sand seas where life will potentially be very difficult," Thomas concluded.

The United Kingdom's charitable Tearfund issued a report showing that some efforts to slow down desertification are taking hold. One example was in Niger, where the people have built low, stone dykes across contours, which have proven to prevent runoff, preserving water for the soil. The people of India's Bihar region have built embankments to connect villages during floods, including culverts to allow for drainage.

Repeated Patterns

The same patterns will be repeated in other deserts on other continents as weather patterns continue to change in reaction to rising global temperatures. The United Nations conducted research on the matter and released the 2006 report *Global Deserts Outlook*, which addresses the issues facing the planet's sandy regions. Already, 10 to 20 percent of the drylands have been classified as degraded, which means their ability to produce crops has been severely reduced.

"The probability of regions in the interiors of continents becoming desert will increase," said Ronald Prinn, codirector of the Joint Program on the Science and Policy of Global Change at the Massachusetts Institute of Technology, in an interview with *Agence France-Presse*.

The Dashti Kbir Desert in Iran was reported by the UN to have lost 16 percent of its annual rainfall over the past twenty-five years, while the Kalahari experienced a 12 percent decline and Chile's Atacama Desert saw an 8 percent drop.

Accompanying the drop in rainfall has been a steady rise in temperatures. The UN's Intergovernmental Panel on Climate Change (IPCC) reported in 2006 that desert temperatures could rise an average of 9° to 12.6° F (5° to 7° C) by 2071 to 2100 compared to the period from 1961 to 1990.

If true, then that equation means increased evaporation of the little moisture extant and a rise in the velocity and frequency of dust storms. People and animals living in the desert will be forced to the land's edges, near more temperate climates.

One major conclusion was that those living in the desert biome will find life increasingly difficult in both the short and long term. One factor was the higher percentage of salt found in water, making

Overdevelopment in deserts around the world will tax the ecosystems.

the land less arable for agriculture and the water less drinkable. The salt content in the water tables found beneath irrigated land has increased, a phenomenon commonly found today throughout China, India, Pakistan, and Australia. The report indicated the Tarm River basin in China has lost more than 5,000 square miles (8,047 sq km) of farmland due to salinization over the past three decades.

Deserts and many rivers derive their water from melting ice and snow atop mountains. As the snowfall decreases given the rising temperatures, less water is available for the normal weather patterns. Asia will be particularly hard hit by these changes with the glaciers covering mountains in the continent's southern quadrant estimated to shrink up to 80 percent over the next one hundred years. That will impact the lives of those living in Bangladesh, Pakistan, India, and China.

Irrigation

Many fast-growing desert communities, such as Phoenix in the United States and Riyadh in Saudi Arabia, are outstripping the land's ability to support so many people. Plans to irrigate the deserts from nearby rivers have proven to be unrealistic.

Water management has been a worldwide concern for some time and is growing in importance as the available drinkable water is threatened by changes in the environment. American towns like Atlanta, Georgia, struggle to provide water to its rising population, while Saudi Arabia was criticized for the choice it made with irrigated fields. Rather than growing wheat, the UN said Saudi Arabia should use the liquid for growing dates.

Changing weather patterns have had some unpredictable effects, such as previously dry areas receiving additional rainfall. One area gaining in precipitation is the Sahara, where vegetation has improved markedly over the past fifteen years, arresting the growth of the desert's southern region. Other portions of the desert biome may shift from dry to wet and become a new biome altogether.

A woman in Israel tends to a vertical garden using methods that coax water from below.

The UN report suggests that the vast desert terrain be harnessed to collect and channel solar energy to address the growing demand for energy. One example provided was that an area of the Sahara desert measuring 250,000 square miles (402,000 sq km) could collect enough solar energy to generate enough electricity for the whole world's current needs.

Additionally, if well planned, the deserts could become popular tourist destinations as people seek exotic vistas. Also, if properly cultivated, desert plant life could become the desirable crops of the future.

Professor Andrew Warren of University College London told *National Geographic*, "We risk losing not only astounding landscapes and ancient cultures but also wild species that may hold keys to our survival."

CHAPTER 5

THE DESERT CHANGES WITH THE WORLD

The desert biome is undergoing dramatic changes now, and those changes are expected to accelerate in the coming century. It's because of global warming and man's attempts to farm or mine the land and build new communities in the harsh environment.

The desert environs have become a magnet for tourists, with Egypt recording a steady increase in visitors over the past decade. The greater number of people and accompanying toxic fumes in the atmosphere from planes, boats, and cars have accelerated the deterioration of many temples, pyramids, and statues that date back thousands of years.

Flush with oil-derived wealth, the United Arab Emirates have become one of the world's fastest-growing tourist destinations, despite the heat and sand.

As more construction is undertaken, the amount of wilderness area is expected to decrease. At the current rates of development, the United Nations predicts that the desert wilderness will drop from 59 percent of total deserts in 2005 to a low of 31 percent by 2050.

Such increased growth will have a hazardous affect on other life in the desert, notably animal life. The desert bighorn sheep, Asian houbara bustard, and desert tortoise are among

the species that may be most adversely affected as rangelands are diminished.

A Fragile Ecology

With people more aware of the fragile ecology, more thought has been going into development, making better use of the meager resources available and importing supplies where possible. There have been great strides made in water extraction and supply technologies, along with greater emphasis on water desalinization efforts. New ways to mine minerals and oil from the land have decreased the harm to the local environs. As some oil supplies near depletion, land reclamation planning has begun, notably in the Middle East.

Still, much damage has been caused to the desert environment because man has treated the biome as a wasteland, not an ecosystem, and tested hazardous materials such as nuclear weapons, which have created long-lasting damage. Some nuclear waste is stored in the desert. Given the dry weather, acres of desert have been turned into parking lots for retired airplanes and military ordnance. All of this has had an impact on life in the area.

GOVERNMENT

In addition to climate changes, the ever-evolving nature of government and commercial forces will also affect how people live in the desert. Trade will most certainly be altered as some deserts get drier and others flourish with newfound rainfall. The same will occur to plant and animal life. One UN report suggests that almost half of the Chihuahuan Desert's bird, mammal, and butterfly species will be replaced by 2055.

Other previous harm done to the biome will take decades or centuries to show recovery, and, by then, global climate changes will mean additional adaptation for both plant and animal life.

Species native to the desert and those from outside the biome cross the land as part of their migratory patterns. With increased development by man, birds and other animals have to compete at oases for water and food. Insects also struggle for survival, and the desert locust, normally found in twenty-five countries in Africa and the Arabian Peninsula, has spread to sixty-five countries. During peak outbreaks, they could consume one hundred thousand tons of vegetation a day and can be found from India to Morocco, in addition to the Caribbean and Venezuela. Their impact can be keenly felt and may increase as they migrate with the changing sands.

Increased Storms

The drier deserts and warmer temperatures will increase windstorms, and with them will be carried sand and minerals from one region to another. This will have its own consequences. Within the dust and sand are nutrients, including phosphorus and silicon, which would enhance oceanic phytoplankton growth that could benefit the productivity of some marine ecosystems. Nutrient-deficient tropical soils would also benefit from minerals contained in soil transported from the African regions.

The increased volume of dust in the air is likely to lead to increased respiratory distress. Additionally, more dust storms would impede transportation on land and in the air, which would be harmful to various economies.

All the changes occurring now and in the future will bring about further alterations to how the ecosystem can or cannot sustain life. As increased livestock farming and greater drought damage the

In the United Arab Emirates, both camels and cars navigate slowly through a heavy sandstorm, a very common occurrence in the Middle East.

desert's vegetation covering, the exposed land is dried out and blown about, changing the local environment and wherever the sand and dirt are deposited. Exposed mining and oil drilling also bring with them environmental damage, including contaminating some of the precious freshwater available. The atmosphere is also polluted, which traps greenhouse gases and dirties the air. This is a growing problem in Argentina and Chile.

Australia introduced their National Soil Conservation Program in 1983, resulting in expanded and improved soil and water conservation technologies across the country. The Australian desert's fish are healthy when compared to conditions that other animal life experiences around the world. One reason they are hardier is that the continent avoided dramatic changes to natural water flow and introduction of species not native to the environment.

Images taken by the Huygens probe show the terrain of Titan, which is Saturn's moon.

Global Attention

Despite regional organizations and even the United Nations' attention devoted to the deserts, a global initiative does not yet exist to address the changes being made to the biome. With each passing year, changes continue and some accelerate with scientists studying these alterations and predicting what will come next.

Interestingly, the Huygens probe aboard the *Cassini* spacecraft that landed on Titan, Saturn's moon, revealed Earth-like conditions that scientists say may be a glimpse of our deserts' future. "Titan may be very different from Earth today, but maybe not Earth tomorrow," Jonathan Lunine, a Cassini-Huygens interdisciplinary scientist at the University of Arizona, told Space.com.

"Rains on deserts on Earth can be spaced by months to years, but on Titan we're talking about hundreds, maybe thousands, of years between episodes of major rainfall that comes down perhaps violently," Lunine said. "Because Titan is so much farther from the sun than Earth is, it takes longer for solar energy to evaporate methane and build it up in the atmosphere enough to generate storms.

"There's a sense here of a desert world. Not in terms of being hot—Titan is very cold—but in terms of being very dry. Titan lacks oceans, but someday Earth will, too, as the sun increases in brightness, boiling the oceans away and leaving Earth a desert planet."

amphibian A cold-blooded animal that has gills and lungs allowing it to operate both on land and in the water.

arroyo A small, deep gully with steep sides; it's dry except during the heavy rainy season.

barchan A sand dune in a crescent shape.

dune A sand hill or ridge shaped and reshaped by wind.

dust devil A whirlwind measuring 10 to 100 feet (3 to 30 m) in diameter and several hundred to 1,000 feet (304 m) high, made visible by the sand.

ecology The interactions between organisms and their environment, including other organisms.

ecosystem The interaction of a community of organisms with their environment.

eluviation The movement through the soil of materials brought into suspension or dissolved by the action of water.

erg A wide spread of land covered with sand.

erosion The process by which land is worn away by water and/ or wind.

hamattan The dry-season weather influenced by winds from the Sahara.

khamsin A southerly wind, blowing southeast to southwest, regularly found in Egypt and the Red Sea about fifty days a year, beginning in the middle of March.

oasis A fertile area, usually having a spring or well.

playa Sandy and/or salty flat floor of a desert basin with interior drainage; it becomes a shallow lake during heavy rains.

santana Hot, dust-bearing winds from the coast to the interior lands, best known in America as the Santa Anas.

sirocco A hot, dry, dust-laden wind blowing from northern Africa and affecting parts of southern Europe.

stomata Any of various small apertures, especially one of the minute orifices or slits in the epidermis of leaves, stems, etc., through which gases are exchanged.

succulent Describing plants with thick, fleshy, water-storing leaves or stems.

wadi A channel that is dry except during periods of rainfall.

water table The underground surface where materials, including soil or rock, are saturated with water.

Desert Research Institute

2215 Raggio Parkway

Reno, NV 89512

(775) 673-7300

Web site: http://www.dri.edu

With offices in Reno, Las Vegas, and Boulder City, this Nevada operation has done extensive research into America's western deserts.

Desert Survivors

P.O. Box 20991

Oakland, CA 94620-0991

(510) 769-1706

Web site: http://www.desert-survivors.org

Desert Survivors is a nonprofit organization founded in 1981 with the mission of experiencing, sharing, and protecting desert wilderness.

DesertUSA

P.O. Box 270219

San Diego, CA 92198-0219

(760) 740-1787 ext. 1

Web site: http://www.desertusa.com

DesertUSA's all-encompassing Web site has details and maps on deserts and their flora and fauna.

The Living Desert

47-900 Portola Avenue

Palm Desert, CA 92260

(760) 346-5694

Web site: http://www.livingdesert.org

This organization is dedicated to desert conservation through preservation, education, and appreciation.

OneWorld Magazine

P.O. Box 49934

Austin, TX 78751

Fax: (512) 451-3879

Web site: http://www.oneworldmagazine.org

OneWord is an electronic magazine about the global environment with articles to educate and entertain readers.

Web Sites

Due to the changing nature of Internet links, Rosen Publishing has developed an online list of Web sites related to the subject of this book. This site is updated regularly. Please use this link to access the list:

http://www.rosenlinks.com/biom/dese

Allaby, Michael, Robert Anderson, and Ian Crofton. *Deserts and Semideserts* (Biomes Atlases). New York, NY: Raintree Books, 2003.

Campbell, David. *The Crystal Desert: Summers in Antarctica*. New York, NY: Mariner Books, 2002.

Davis, Barbara J. *Biomes and Ecosystems*. Strongsville, OH: Gareth Stevens Publishing, 2007.

Eigeland, Tor, et al. *The Desert Realm*. Washington, DC: National Geographic, 1982.

Johnson, Mark. *The Ultimate Desert Handbook: A Manual for Desert Hikers, Campers and Travelers*. Thomaston, ME: International Marine/Ragged Mountain Press, 2003.

MacMahon, James A. *Deserts*. New York, NY: Alfred A. Knopf, 1985.

Ricciuti, Edward R. *Desert* (Biomes of the World). New York, NY: Benchmark Books, 1996.

Warhol, Tom. *Desert* (Earth's Biomes). New York, NY: Benchmark Books, 2006.

BIBLIOGRAPHY

Adam, David. "Global Warming Could End Sahara Droughts, Says Study." *The Guardian*, September 16, 2005. Retrieved January 3, 2008 (http://www.guardian.co.uk/science/2005/sep/16/highereducation.climatechange).

Allaby, Michael. *Biomes of the World: Volume Two—Deserts.* Danbury, CT: Grolier Publishing Company, 1999.

Barramedasoft Corporation. "Deserts." Retrieved January 3, 2008 (http://www.barrameda.com.ar/ecology/the-deserts.htm).

Black, Richard. "Climate Water Threat to Millions." BBC News, October 20, 2006. Retrieved January 3, 2008 (http://news.bbc.co.uk/2/hi/science/nature/6068348.stm).

Center for Educational Technologies. "Biomes: Desert." April 28, 2005. Retrieved January 3, 2008 (http://www.cotf.edu/ete/modules/msese/earthsysflr/desert.html).

Chaon, Anne, and Richard Ingham. "Global Warming and Deserts Are a Double-Edged Sword." TerraDaily.com, June 20, 2006. Retrieved January 3, 2008 (http://www.terradaily.com/reports/Global_Warming_And_Deserts_Are_A_Double_Edged_Sword.html).

Choi, Charles Q. "Titan May Foreshadow Earth's Desert Future." MSNBC.com, June 12, 2007. Retrieved January 3, 2008 (http://www.msnbc.msn.com/id/19188532/).

DesertUSA.com. "Deserts." 2008. Retrieved January 3, 2008 (http://www.desertusa.com/).

Dixon, Dougal. *Deserts and Wastelands.* London, UK: Aladdin Books, 1984.

Information Please Database. "Principal Deserts of the World." 2007. Retrieved January 3, 2008 (http://www.infoplease.com/ipa/A0778851.html).

Jenkins, Martin. *Endangered People and Places: Deserts.* Minneapolis, MN: Lerner Publishing Company, 1995.

Lovgren, Stefan. "Global Warming May Unleash 'Sand Seas' in Africa, Model Shows." NationalGeographic.com, June 29, 2005. Retrieved January 3, 2008 (http://news.nationalgeographic.com/news/2005/06/0629_050629_dunes.html).

Missouri Botanical Garden. "Deserts." 2002. Retrieved January 3, 2008 (http://www.mbgnet.net/sets/desert/index.htm).

NASA. "Desert." Retrieved January 3, 2008 (http://earthobservatory.nasa.gov/Laboratory/Biome/biodesert.html).

Perry, Richard. *Life in Desert and Plain*. New York, NY: Taplinger Publishing Company, 1977.

Soojung-Kim Pang, Alex. "Desert Cities and Climate Change." Institute for the Future, June 4, 2006. Retrieved January 3, 2008 (http://future.iftf.org/2006/06/desert_cities_a.html).

University of California Museum of Paleontology. "The Desert Biome." Retrieved January 3, 2008 (http://www.ucmp.berkeley.edu/exhibits/biomes/deserts.php).

United Nations Environment Programme. *The Global Deserts Outlook*. Retrieved January 3, 2008 (http://www.unep.org/geo/gdoutlook/).

Urban Development for You. "What Is a Desert?" Retrieved January 3, 2008 (http://library.thinkquest.org/J0110521/what_is_a_desert.htm).

U.S. Geological Survey. "What Is a Desert?" December 18, 2001. Retrieved January 3, 2008 (http://pubs.usgs.gov/gip/deserts/what/).

Vogelgesang, Jennifer. *Discovering Deserts*. Lincolnwood, IL: Publishing International Limited, 1992.

WorldBiomes.com. "Desert Biomes." January 22, 2002. Retrieved January 3, 2008 (http://www.worldbiomes.com/biomes_desert.htm).

INDEX

A

adaptation, 5, 23, 24, 27, 36
Arabian Desert, 18
arroyos, 11
Atacama Desert, 10, 12, 29, 31

B

biomes, 5, 6, 31, 33, 34, 36, 38

C

cactus/cacti, 8, 20–21, 22, 23
camels, 24
Chihuahuan Desert, 35
Colorado Great Basin, 17, 29

D

Dashti Kbir Desert, 31
Death Valley, 15
desertification, 6, 12, 14, 29, 30
deserts
    animal life in, 5, 11, 14, 20, 24–26, 27, 30, 31, 34–35, 36
    classification of, 8–9
    cold, 14, 19, 27
    formation of, 6, 7, 10–11
    and global warming, 5, 28–33, 34, 36
    locations of, 7, 9, 10–11, 14, 27
    people in, 5, 10, 11, 15, 16, 17, 20, 26–27, 28, 30, 31, 32–33, 35
    plant life in, 5, 8, 11, 14, 17, 20–23, 26, 27, 31, 33, 35, 36–37
    preconceptions about, 5, 14
    preservation of, 34–38

    rainfall in, 5, 6, 8–9, 11, 14, 17, 21, 22, 28, 30, 31, 33
    and space exploration, 6, 12, 38
    temperature in, 5, 8, 15, 24, 27, 31, 34, 36
    topography of, 7, 10, 16–17, 22, 28–30
    and tourism, 33, 34
    types of, 7, 8–9, 14, 15–19, 27
    water sources in, 8, 11–12, 17, 18, 26, 32, 35, 36, 37
desert winds, types of, 16
drought, 28, 29
drylands, 8–9, 12, 31
Dust Bowl, 14
dust devils, 16
dust storms, 36

E

ecosystems, 5, 11, 14, 21, 26, 35, 36
ecozones, 17–19
evaporation, 9, 11, 12, 21, 22, 31

F

flash floods, 11
flatlands, 15, 16
frilled lizards, 26

G

Global Deserts Outlook, 31
global warming, 5, 28–33, 34, 36
Gobi Desert, 29
Great Victorian Desert, 29

H

hardpan, 12

About the Author

Robert Greenberger is a writer and journalist who has covered a wide variety of nonfiction topics, notably popular culture. His work has appeared in *Analog*, *Heavy Metal*, *Starlog*, *Worlds of If*, *Video Games*, *Sci-Fi Universe*, *Sci-Fi Channel*, and *Back Issue*. He makes his home in Connecticut.

Photo Credits

Cover © www.istockphoto.com/Robert Bremec; cover (inset), p. 1 © www.istockphoto.com/David Gunn; pp. 4–5 Jenny Acheson/Axiom/Getty Images; pp. 8, 11, 18, 21, 23, 37 Shutterstock.com; p. 9 Michael & Patricia Fogden/Minden Pictures/Getty Images; pp. 13, 30 © AP Images; p. 16 Stan Osolinski/Taxi/Getty Images; p. 25 © www.istockphoto.com/Nico Smit; p. 26 © Zigmund Leszczynski/Animals Animals—Earth Scenes; p. 27 Doug Allen/Stone/Getty Images; p. 29 © www.istockphoto.com/Viktor Glupov; p. 32 © www.istockphoto.com/Halder Yousuf; p. 33 David Doubilet/National Geographic/Getty Images; p. 38 NASA; back cover inset images (left to right) © www.istockphoto.com/Lilli Day, © www.istockphoto.com/Maceofoto, © www.istockphoto.com/David Gunn, © www.istockphoto.com/Paul Senyszyn, © www.istockphoto.com/John Anderson, © www.istockphoto.com/TT.

Designer: Les Kanturek; Editor: Nicholas Croce
Photo Researcher: Amy Feinberg